Four Seasons of Roses

Monthly Guide to Rose Care

By Susan Fox

Like us on Facebook at
www.facebook.com/gagasgarden
Follow me on twitter @gagasgarden

For more images exclusively by Susan Fox visit:

www.istockphoto.com/portfolio/gagasgarden

www.gagasgarden.com

Four Seasons of Roses Planner: Monthly Guide to Rose Care offers you four full seasons of enjoyment. Each month there are things-to-do to establish and maintain a beautiful rose garden. Gardeners enjoy planning, learning about and being in their garden. The *Four Seasons of Roses Planner* will help you establish your unique garden history to learn and grow your knowledge base each year. As you write your garden diary notes you can reflect back on what works best for your garden and microclimate each year. Over the years, people have told me they desire roses in their garden. My *Four Seasons of Roses Planner* is an easy to follow monthly guide in knowing *what-to-do* to grow beautiful roses. Every rose featured in this garden planner, I carefully selected, planted, nurtured and photographed in my Central, Illinois rose garden-Gaga's Garden®. This planner will inspire you and gardeners everywhere to add roses to your gardens with simple steps each month to follow. For more in-depth information regarding scheduling Susan as a speaker, event planner or bringing a rose garden to your city contact Susan Fox at www.gagasgarden.com.

All Images featured in this planner are original artwork by Susan Fox:

www.istockphoto.com/portfolio/gagasgarden

Susan Fox, Consulting Rosarian

Cover Rose: 'Blake Hedrick' HT

January

January is a great month for rose shopping. You can shop online or from your rose catalogs. Most rose nursery catalogs are now online so you can preview the roses and read about them to determine which selections would be best for your garden. Go to plantmaps.com and determine the last possible date in your zone for a hard freeze. Most rose providers will also assist you in determining your zone and ship at the appropriate time.

January is a good month for planning spring gardens and transplanting dormant roses of all types in warmer climates. Be sure to remove soil from the roots and then handle the plant as you would any new bare root rose.

Construction and renovation of existing beds can be planned or completed. Now is a good time to send off soil samples for analysis if you use soil samples in your rose program.

January is a good time to visit www.ars.org and check out all the member benefits. I want to encourage you to find your local society and go to a meeting. Rosarians are committed to assisting you with rose education and sharing their knowledge about roses.

Pictured: 'Rosie O'Donnell' HT

January

Sunday	Monday	Tuesday	Wednesday	Thursday	Friday	Saturday

Notes

February

Go to www.plantmaps.com to determine your USDA plant hardiness zone. I like plant maps because it will tell you all the data you need to know about the last possible date of a hard freeze in your area. If you live in a warmer climate February is a good month to plant rose bushes. I caution about planting too early and risking a loss of tender plants to a late hard freeze.

If new bushes arrive early and must be planted, soak them in plain water to keep the roots from drying out. Up to overnight is fine. Once planted, cover and protect them from freezing with dirt and/or mulch and leaves.

February can be a good time to start cleaning-up around your beds and deciding on your maintenance program and what organic soil amendments you will be adding. Be sure your inventory is sufficient and order if you have not done so.

I've found the local feed store is a great source for organic soil amendments such as cottonseed meal, alfalfa meal, and feather meal.

Be sure to check beds for moisture levels and water if necessary.

Pictured: 'Love Song' F

February

Sunday	Monday	Tuesday	Wednesday	Thursday	Friday	Saturday

Notes

March

Start removing the mulch and dirt from around your rose bushes by using a slow flow from the water hose. It's best to remove the winter protection gradually. Use the entire month to remove the mulch and dirt so that by the end of March the bud union is fully exposed to the sun. The warmth of the sun promotes new canes and basal breaks to grow.

This is when you place a heaping tablespoon of Epsom salt around each bush and water it in well to help promote basal breaks. It's best to have a minimum of three healthy canes or basil breaks on hybrid teas, grandifloras and old garden roses. Five healthy canes are the minimum you want to see on floribundas and miniatures. For shaping purposes and exposing the bud union of the plant to the sun you may have to remove inside canes especially on miniatures and floribundas.

You may find aphids on your plants in early spring. I have found a water wand will wash away aphids. This is a good time to release natural predators in your garden like ladybugs that eat aphids.

It's time to start your feeding program if you have not done so already. If your program has worked in the past stick with it. It's best to feed often in small amounts. This is especially true in extreme heat during the summer months and applies to all types of roses. Water as often as needed.

Pictured: 'California Dreamin' HT

March

Sunday	Monday	Tuesday	Wednesday	Thursday	Friday	Saturday

Notes

April

As a responsible rosarian, determine a program that is safe for the environment and the pests that you may encounter and set it in action on a regular basis. Most chewing insects can be washed away with a water wand without harming good insects and upsetting the balance of nature.

Water as often as needed. Deep watering of about three gallons per week on a large rose bush is sufficient. Raised or elevated rose beds that are comprised of one-third to one-half organic matter are almost impossible to over-water because they have excellent drainage properties.

April is the month to disbud and finger prune varieties that you may be entering in area rose shows. Go to www.ars.org and locate your nearest rose society and check with the consulting rosarians in your society to determine the length of time it takes for certain varieties to bloom so you know when to cut back for a show.

This is when thrips may arrive. Check on the most environmentally responsible way to control them.

Pictured: 'Moondance' F

April

Sunday	Monday	Tuesday	Wednesday	Thursday	Friday	Saturday

Notes

May

Continue your feeding and watering programs. Blooms last longer when a plant is hydrated, therefore it is important to water more just before a rose show.

Continue checking for pests. Check for thrips daily. As the weather gets hotter be on the lookout for spider mites. These mites look like salt and pepper on the underside of leaves. They can be washed away with a high power water wand. Add at least 2 inches of mulch to your beds to retain moisture during the hottest season of summer.

May is also a good time to set up your automatic sprinkler system if you haven't already done so. Be sure to read the manual, most systems are designed to be simple to operate. Some sprinkler systems are designed to have rain sensors and turn off when it rains. If not, be sure to turn them off when it rains.

This is the time to add several inches of fresh mulch around each rose bush. Mulch retains moisture in your garden. Soil polymers can also be added at this time. Soil polymers are a soil amendment designed to reduce plant watering by 50%, as well as reduce transplant shock, soil compaction, and will remain effective in the soil for 3-5 years. This can be an inexpensive way to help the plant retain moisture and is environmentally friendly.

Pictured: 'Garden Party' HT

May

Sunday **Monday** **Tuesday** **Wednesday** **Thursday** **Friday** **Saturday**

Notes

June

Continue all of your programs outlined for May. Cut spent blooms, a process called deadheading, regularly. Mulch is absolutely necessary to retain moisture for the heat of summer. A depth of three or four inches is not too much if the mulch permits water and air to penetrate to the soil. Hardwood mulch is best because of its organic properties that break down to create nutrients and feed the soil. Every day watch your opening buds and blooms. Thrips can spoil blooms rapidly.

June is the month throughout most zones in the US where temperatures begin to soar. During spring months, in many areas, you may have depended on rain for water. Now is the time to be sure to check your watering systems. Dehydration during summer months can put your plants in peril. If you have an irrigation system in place be sure that it's set to water at least 2 inches of water per week. This is difficult to determine when you take into consideration factors like wind, temperature and type of soil so here's a handy chart that may help you decide how to water when the temperatures rise.

Rose Watering Chart Gauge by Temperature
90+ degrees: Water every day
80 degrees: Water every two days
70 degrees: Water every three days
60 degrees: Water every four days
50 degrees: Water every five days

Pictured: 'Easy Does It' F

June

Sunday	Monday	Tuesday	Wednesday	Thursday	Friday	Saturday

Notes

July

Replace mulch as needed. Mulch is a moisture barrier and it keeps beds cooler while preserving moisture. Continue regular feeding and watering programs. Container plants, potted roses, and hanging baskets will need water almost daily. Continue with your maintenance programs for deadheading. Deadheading is the removal of spent blooms forcing the plant to re-bloom. You are removing the blossom before it has had a chance to develop a fruit or plant seed. To deadhead, cut the spent bloom down to the first or second five leaf set that is growing outwards. When you deadhead leave as much foliage as possible since it requires leaves to produce more blooms.

Also, this is a month to keep an eye out for spider mites. You can see spider mites on the under side of leaves with a magnifying glass, or feel them if you rub your fingers on the underside of the leaves. They appear like specks of salt and pepper. If you see webbing in the garden, chances are you have spider mites. Use your water wand and wash the under side of leaves well.

You may notice as temperatures rise that your roses will continue to bloom, however the blooms may be somewhat smaller and a little less frequent. Continue your feeding and watering program to ensure a beautiful fall bloom.

Pictured: 'Fourth of July' LCl

July 2014

Sunday	Monday	Tuesday	Wednesday	Thursday	Friday	Saturday

Notes

August

Watering may be the most important thing you do during August. Continue with your feeding program. If you go on vacation be sure to have someone you trust water for you. Be especially mindful of area water restrictions and remember that roses can get by on 3-5 gallons per plant each week depending on how much dehydration and mulch you have in place. If you see spider mites, remember that a water wand is the best way to wash them away with a strong stream on the underside of the foliage. If you are showing in the fall this is when you will want to disbud and finger prune for any fall shows.

Have you wondered what a Consulting Rosarian (CR) is? A CR is a person who has knowledge about growing roses and the culture of roses. CR is a designation given by the American Rose Society after certain rigorous qualifications have been met. A CR signs an oath to assist gardeners and fellow rosarians in growing roses while spreading the good news that roses are easy to grow and maintain when proper techniques are maintained.

Most rose shows have a novice class in which beginning rose gardeners can enter and show roses. Why don't you call an area CR and ask about showing your roses in the novice class in the fall show?

Pictured Double Delight, HT

August

Sunday	Monday	Tuesday	Wednesday	Thursday	Friday	Saturday

Notes

September

Check for thrips regularly if you intend to exhibit in the local rose show. The nights begin to get cooler this month in most climates, which can create an environment for mildew and black spot. Check for an environmentally safe solution and follow a program to reduce the risk of black spot and mildew until the first frost.

Continue watering deep. Make your last fertilization this month. Continue to cut spent blooms. Those not cut will form rose hips signaling the bush to begin the process of transitioning into a slow dormancy for the winter months.

Think about all the things you can do with your roses:

Rose Photography, Crafting, Collecting, Cooking and Floral Design. You can use the petals this month from the roses you collect to make potpourri. I like this recipe:

5 cups rose petals, ½ cup lavender, 1 T orange peel, 1 cup rose leaves, 1 T allspice, 2 T each of cloves, cinnamon and nutmeg, 2 T gum benzoin or ores root, 5 drops each of rose geranium, patchouli and rosemary, 10 drops rose oil

Place in a crock or tightly closed jar in a dark place for three weeks.

Pictured: 'Julia Child' F

September

Sunday	Monday	Tuesday	Wednesday	Thursday	Friday	Saturday

Notes

October

Do not feed this month or until spring. Continue watering and your responsible maintenance program for black spot until frost or as long as you are getting new growth. After cutting blooms for rose shows, cut blooms only for special occasions allowing the bushes to continue to make rosehips and enter full dormancy for the winter months.

Autumn is the end of the rose garden bloom cycle. It's time for your roses to go into winter dormancy and make rose hips* Allowing your roses to form rosehips helps to "harden" them off for winter. While your roses are "resting," you can take care of your gardening to-do list. Your plants can be reduced in height to waist high to prevent breakage from winter winds. Leave your climbing roses tall but secure them to a trellis or fence. You can cut any leggy branches from tree roses to shape them.

*Rose hips (the fruit of the rose which forms at base of the flower) are a nutritional treasure chest - rich in vitamins (C, E, and K), pectin, beta-carotene, and bioflavonoids. These elements produce a strong antioxidant effect, which protects and enhances the immune system. Rose hips improve blood cholesterol and pressure, digestive efficiency, and weight management (and are also a special winter treat for birds and wild animals).

Pictured: 'Ingrid Bergman' HT

October

Sunday	Monday	Tuesday	Wednesday	Thursday	Friday	Saturday

Notes

November

Water as needed. Do not feed. Be sure all your winter protection is in place. Store all of your materials and label them. Clean and oil all of your tools for storage. Now is a good time to organize your garden shed so you know what you may need to re-order for spring.

Roses planted in containers should be moved closer to the house. If you live in an extreme climate, you will need to take action to protect your roses for the winter.

Planting and transplanting roses can be done successfully during the fall. Carefully prepare the new spot 16" deep, enriched with the soil amendments I've referenced for spring. For transplanting: carefully place spade 10" from base of plant, dig straight down into the bed in a circle around the plant, trying not to cut roots. Lift the plant with the shovel and carry it directly to the new spot. Fill in soil and cover the plant with a mound of mulch. Water 3-5 gal.

November is a good time to make plans for new rose beds next spring. Prepare the soil for winter or spring plantings now and the soil has time to set and stabilize. Rototill the soil 16" deep and add your soil amendments.

Pictured: 'Oh My!' F

November

Sunday	Monday	Tuesday	Wednesday	Thursday	Friday	Saturday

Notes

December

This is the perfect time to order your rose catalogs. Make a diary of the year on how your roses performed. Review your past eleven months activities and make plans for the coming season. Go online and shop for your roses for spring. It's not too early to place your spring order. Pay your American Rose Society (www.ars.org) dues. Continue to water. If you live in a climate where the ground doesn't freeze this remains a 12-month process.

Modern roses (e.g. hybrid tea, floribunda and grandiflora) need protection from the cold primarily due to the graft union. Carefully remove all plant debris around the base of the plant before applying mulch. Troublesome diseases such as black spot may be present in this debris and will serve as a source of infection the next growing season. Diseased leaves that remain on the rose plant need to be removed as well.

The timing of rose winterization is important. Winterize your roses after several "hard" frosts have occurred but before the soil freezes. This will prevent stem cankers that can occur if you winterize too early while the ground is still warm. Treating the stems with a fungicide used to control black spot of roses before mounding is a good precautionary measure.

Pictured: 'Iceberg' F

December

Sunday	Monday	Tuesday	Wednesday	Thursday	Friday	Saturday

Notes

www.ingramcontent.com/pod-product-compliance
Lightning Source LLC
Chambersburg PA
CBHW041753040426
42446CB00001B/21